# WONDERFUL
## World

### NICOLA BAXTER

TWO CAN™

LONDON ▪ PRINCETON

# How to use this book

## Cross references
Above the heading on the page, you will find a list of subjects in the book which are connected to the topic. Look up these pages to find out more about the subjects.

## See for yourself
See for yourself bubbles give you the chance to test out some of the ideas in this book. They explain what you will need and what you have to do to see if an idea really works.

## Quiz corner
In the quiz corner, you will find a list of questions. The answers to the quiz questions are somewhere on the two pages. Can you answer all the questions about each topic?

## Glossary
Difficult words are explained in the glossary near the back of the book. These words are in **bold** on the page. Look them up in the glossary to find out what they mean.

## Index
The index is at the back of the book. It is a list of words about everything mentioned in the book, with page numbers next to the words. The list is in the same order as the alphabet. If you want to find out about a subject, look up the word in the index, then turn to the page number given.

# Contents

# Planet Earth

Our **planet** Earth is never still. It is moving and changing all the time. We cannot feel it, but our planet is similar to a ball spinning in space. It is not floating freely but follows a set path round the nearest star, which is the Sun. In turn, a smaller ball, called the Moon, moves steadily round the Earth.

**The Earth**
The Earth travels round, or **orbits**, the Sun in just over 365 days, which is one year. At the same time as the Earth orbits the Sun, it is also spinning round like a top. It makes one complete turn every 24 hours.

Moon's path round the Earth .......

Earth....

Moon .......

▶ When astronauts move far enough away from Earth and escape the **force** of **gravity**, they float.

**Gravity**
The Earth and Sun pull things towards them with a force called gravity. Gravity keeps everything, including people, trees, rocks and water, pulled down on to the Earth's surface, so that they do not float off into space.

**The Moon**
The Moon travels round the Earth once every four weeks. On its way, it seems to change shape, from a circle to a thin curve, or crescent. This is because the Sun lights up different parts of the Moon as it makes its journey.

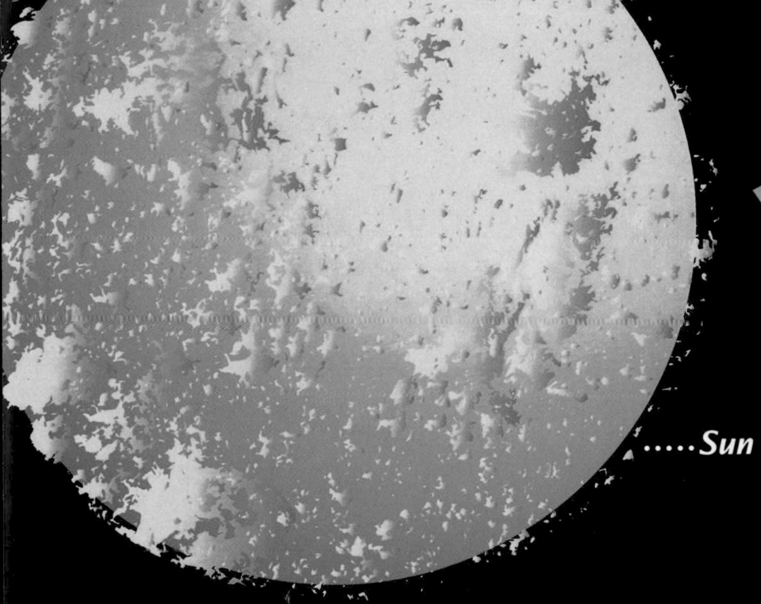

.....Sun

## The Sun

The Sun is really a huge ball of fire. All the Earth's heat and light comes from the Sun. Living things cannot survive without it.

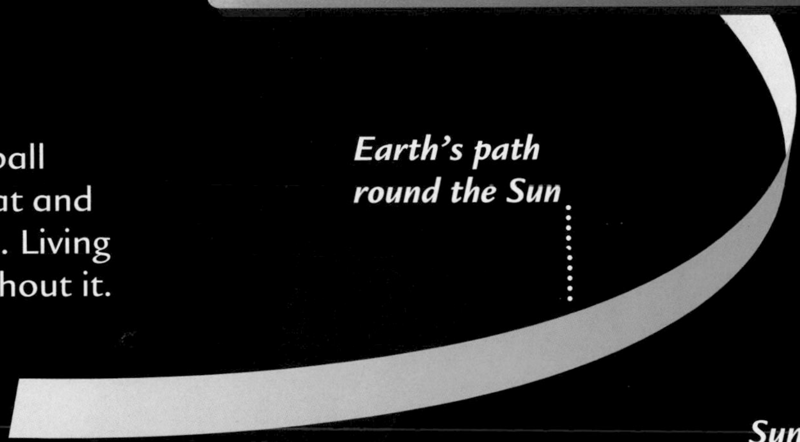

*Earth's path round the Sun*

*Sun......*

## The Sun and Earth

The widest and hottest part of the Earth is round its middle. We draw an imaginary line here and call it the **equator**.

When your part of the Earth is turned towards the Sun, it is day. When it is turned away, it is night.

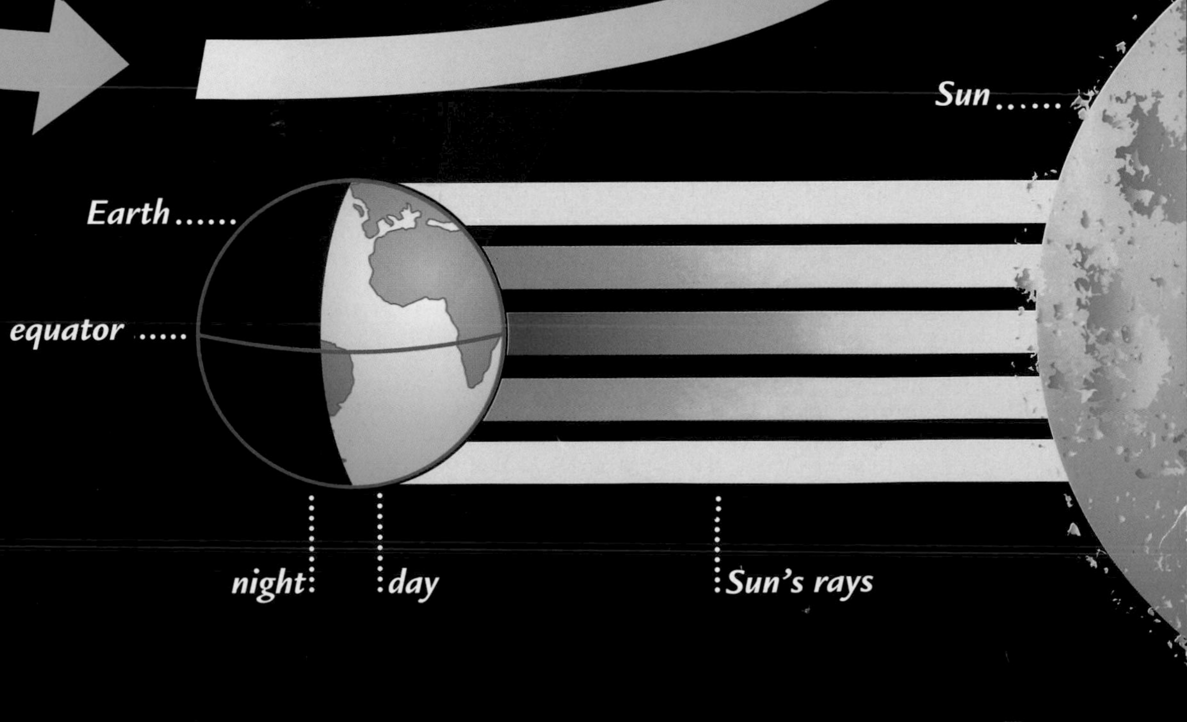

*Earth......*

*equator .....*

*night*  *day*  *Sun's rays*

look at: Volcanoes, page 8, Earthquakes, page 10

#  Inside the Earth

The Earth is made up of layers. Beneath the top layers, there are metals and rocks that are so hot they have melted, or become **molten**. The top layers can tell us what the Earth was like millions of years ago. These layers are changing all the time.

*The **crust** is made up of rocks and soil. This layer and the top part of the **mantle** float on the molten layer below.*

*The mantle is under the crust. It is made of rock, which is so hot parts of it are moving slowly.*

mantle

outer core

inner core

crust

*The outer **core** is made of molten metal, most of which is iron.*

**The moving Earth**
Millions of years ago, all the land on Earth was one huge **continent**. Gradually the land moved apart. Today, it is still moving very slowly.

*the world today*

*millions of years ago*

*The inner core is a solid ball of metal which is extremely hot.*

## The secrets of rock

Beneath the soil, there is solid rock which in some places pokes above ground. Millions of years ago, some of this rock was molten and flowed over the ground. Then it slowly cooled. Above the rock, there is a layer of subsoil.

▶ The Earth's crust is made up of layers. The layer we know best, called soil, is home to many living things.

## Secret fossils

Sometimes, when rocks are forming, a plant or the body of an animal can be trapped between the layers. When the plant or animal rots away, it leaves a space behind. This space slowly fills up with rock, making a copy of the plant or animal, called a **fossil**.

▶ The fossilized shell of an **extinct** creature called an ammonite looks a bit like a Catherine wheel.

soil ...
plant ...
roots ...
subsoil ....
hard rock ...

▼ Underground there are metals and gems. These can be made into jewellery.

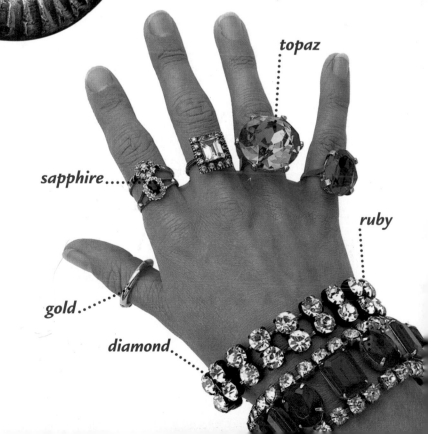

topaz
sapphire ....
ruby
gold ...
diamond ...

## Quiz Corner

● What is the top layer of the Earth called?

● What is the name of a rock that is the same shape as the body of a living thing from long ago?

● How many continents were there millions of years ago?

look at: Inside the Earth, page 6, Mountains, page 14

# Volcanoes

A volcano is a mountain that has gases and hot liquid rock, called lava, inside it. When **pressure** builds up inside the volcano, the gases and lava erupt, or explode, from the top. An **extinct** volcano will never erupt again, but an active volcano may be quiet for many years, then suddenly erupt.

▼ Japanese Macaque monkeys enjoy bathing in hot pools.

### Inside a volcano

Over many years, a volcano builds up from layers of ash and lava that flow down from the opening, or vent. The ash and lava cool and become rock. This is why many volcanoes are cone-shaped.

vent        lava

### Geysers and hot pools

Sometimes underground lakes and rivers pass over **molten** lava. When this happens, water is heated under **pressure** and may suddenly spurt up in a hot fountain, called a geyser, or bubble up into hot pools.

## SEE FOR YOURSELF

*You can see what happens when gases are put under pressure by shaking a plastic bottle half full of fizzy drink. Be very careful as you take the top off, because the liquid inside acts just like the lava in a volcano!*

▼ Volcanoes throw out dust and ash as well as molten lava. This makes it difficult for plants and animals to live on the slopes of active volcanoes.

## Quiz Corner

● What is the hot, liquid rock inside a volcano called?

● What happens when rivers pass over molten lava?

● Why don't many plants and animals live on active volcanoes?

● What shape are most volcanoes?

look at: Inside the Earth, page 6

# Earthquakes

An earthquake happens when rocks move along cracks in the Earth's **crust**. This can make the crust shake and break. The shaking may be so slight that you can hardly feel it, or it may cause buildings to fall to the ground. When earthquakes happen under the sea, they sometimes make enormous waves, called tsunami.

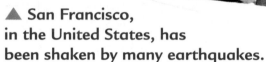

▲ San Francisco, in the United States, has been shaken by many earthquakes.

### Fault lines

Usually, earthquakes happen at places where there is a break in the Earth's crust, called a fault. Most parts of the Earth do not have earthquakes.

▲ The San Andreas fault, in the western United States, can be seen clearly from the air.

**CHATTERBOX**

Animals often warn people that an earthquake is coming. Usually quiet animals become restless. Geese honk noisily and other birds fly round in circles.

## Standing firm

To make sure that a building can stay standing during an earthquake, builders put metal rods inside concrete building blocks. They also leave enough space for the walls of the building to move a little. This means that even tall skyscrapers can be built in areas where there may be earthquakes.

▶ The Transamerica Pyramid, in San Francisco, is a modern building that can remain standing during an earthquake.

### Measuring earthquakes

Scientists use the Mercalli scale to describe what happens in an earthquake. This scale is named after an Italian scientist.

*At scale 4, windows, pots and pans rattle and wooden door frames creak.*

*At scale 6, furniture moves about, windows break and cracks appear in walls.*

*At scale 8, bridges and chimneys may fall. Buildings move on their foundations.*

*At scale 10, most buildings cannot stand. Many trees fall down.*

## Quiz Corner

● What are broken places in the Earth's crust called?

● What is the name of the scale we use to describe what happens during an earthquake?

● What can happen when there is an earthquake under the sea?

look at: Rivers and lakes, page 16

# Land shapes

The shape of the land is changing all the time. Natural **forces**, including wind, water and ice, can wear away rocks, mountains and soil. This is called **erosion**. These changes happen gradually, over many years.

**Caves**
Rainwater and underground rivers can **erode** rocks, forming caves which become homes for bats and birds. When water drips from the roof of a cave, **chemicals** in the water can make long rock shapes grow from the ceiling. These are called stalactites. Similar shapes standing on the floor are called stalagmites.

**Land shaped by water**
When water rushes through rocks, it carves out a path for itself. Over millions of years, this path can become a deep **valley**. The Grand Canyon, in the United States, was made by the Colorado River, which cut through rocks that are up to 2,000 million years old. The Grand Canyon is 446km long and 1.5km deep.

▲ Over millions of years, Antelope Canyon in Arizona, in the United States, was formed by water carving a path through pink sandstone rock.

## Ice ages

Several times in the past, large parts of the Earth have been covered with ice. When huge sheets of the ice, called **glaciers,** moved, they pushed rocks and soil in front of them, making valleys and hills.

▼ There are still glaciers today, moving slowly and gradually changing the landscape.

▲ Long ago, rivers carved out strange-shaped hills in Monument Valley, in the United States. Today, the land is desert, but wind-blown sand still rubs away the rocks.

### CHATTERBOX

The strong roots of a plant growing in a tiny crack in a rock can split the rock wide open.

## Quiz Corner

- What is the long rock shape hanging from the roof of a cave called?
- Which river made the Grand Canyon in the United States?
- What is a huge sheet of ice called?
- Which part of a plant can split a rock?

look at: Inside the Earth, page 6, Volcanoes, page 8

# Mountains

Mountain ranges are strips of high land. They are made slowly over millions of years. In some places, mountains have formed when one part of the Earth's **crust** has pushed against another part, making huge folds of rock. In other places, the Earth's crust has broken into blocks, which have moved up or down to make new mountains.

▼ The longest mountain range in the world is the Andes, which runs down the western side of the **continent** of South America.

## SEE FOR YOURSELF

*Roll out three thick layers of Plasticine and place them one on top of the other. Cut through the layers to make a strip about 20cm long. Push the ends of the strip until the middle rises and folds. The coloured layers show the shapes of the rocks inside "fold" mountains.*

**The highest mountains**
The Himalayan mountain range, in central Asia, is the highest in the world. The range was formed when parts of the Earth's crust pushed against each other, squeezing up the rock.

## Cold on top

Towards the top of a mountain, the **temperature** drops. This means that even in hot parts of the world, mountain tops are covered with ice and snow. Few plants and animals can survive on the cold higher mountain slopes. Plants grow near the ground to avoid the icy winds.

▲ Llamas are one of the most useful animals to the mountain peoples of South America. They can carry heavy loads along the mountain paths and their thick wool can be made into warm clothes.

## Quiz Corner

● What is a strip of high land called?

● Where are the highest mountains in the world?

● What is the name of the longest mountain range in the world?

● Which animal is important to the mountain peoples of South America?

look at: Mountains, page 14, Oceans, page 18

# Rivers and lakes

The beginning of a river is called its source. Often, a river begins from a mountain spring. The water from the spring flows down the mountain and finds the easiest path across the land to the sea. As the river flows along, it carves out a path for itself, carrying soil and even rocks with it.

## CHATTERBOX

In Scotland, some people say they have seen a monster in a lake called Loch Ness. The loch is extremely deep, so it is difficult to prove whether the monster, known as Nessie, exists or not.

▲ Rivers are important because they bring water to farmland. The mouth of a river is where it flows into a large lake or the sea.

## Waterfalls

When water tumbles over a huge step of rock, it makes a waterfall. The water flows over hard rock and **erodes** soft rock below. Sometimes the soft rock is so eroded, the hard rock at the top of the waterfall hangs forward.

▲ At Iguazu Falls in South America, the **force** of the water wears away the rocks.

▶ Big rocks in a river make water splash and swirl into white water. Many people enjoy paddling rafts over this fast-flowing water.

### Oxbow lakes

An oxbow lake is made when the path of a river changes course. A big bend in a river can become a lake when the river flows straight on, leaving its bend cut off by a bank of soil.

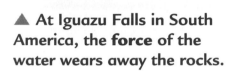

river.....

oxbow lake

river

bank of soil

## Quiz Corner

● What is the beginning of a river called?

● What shape is an oxbow lake?

● What makes river water swirl into white water?

● Where do rivers often begin from?

look at: Mountains, page 14, Rivers and lakes, page 16

# Oceans

Most of our **planet** Earth is covered by water and not by land. Four large oceans and many smaller seas cover over half of the Earth. These oceans and seas are not still. The water flows backwards and forwards in movements, called **tides**. At high tide, the water moves further on to the land. At low tide, it falls back again. The wind also moves the water into waves which rise up and fall down.

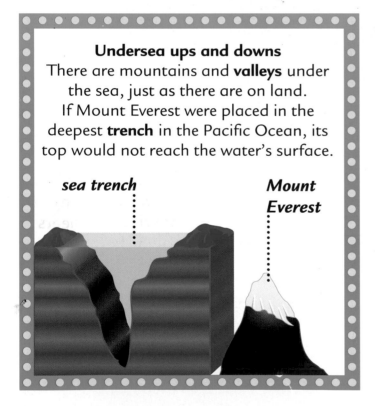

**Undersea ups and downs**
There are mountains and **valleys** under the sea, just as there are on land.
If Mount Everest were placed in the deepest **trench** in the Pacific Ocean, its top would not reach the water's surface.

*sea trench*

*Mount Everest*

### Oceans
The four oceans of the world are called the Pacific Ocean, the Atlantic Ocean, the Indian Ocean and the Arctic Ocean. The largest of these is the Pacific Ocean.

**CHATTERBOX**

It is easier to float in the sea than in fresh water because seawater is salty. The saltiest sea in the world is the Dead Sea in Israel.

▶ The wind can make huge waves crash on to the beach. Many people enjoy surfing on these waves.

## Wind and waves

When the wind blows across the sea, it whips the water into waves. A little breeze can cause ripples, while a gale can make huge waves. Seawater looks as if it is moving along, but it is really moving up and down. It's only where the sea meets the land that waves roll in towards the shore.

▲ Oceans are home to millions of living things. These fish are looking for food in a coral reef. The reef looks like a plant, but really is made from small sea animals.

## Quiz Corner

● Where is the water at high tide?

● Which is the largest ocean?

● Where is the saltiest sea in the world?

● How much of our planet Earth is covered by oceans and seas?

look at: Land shapes, page 12, Oceans, page 18

# Polar lands

There are huge areas of snow and ice at the far north and far south of the Earth. These are called the North and South Poles. They are the coldest places on Earth.

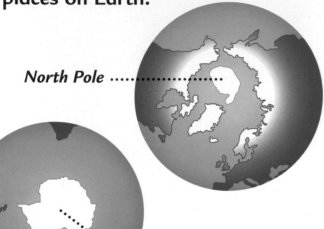

North Pole ......

South Pole

**Iceberg secrets**
Sometimes enormous chunks of ice break free from the frozen sea and float away. These icebergs look enormous, but only a small part can be seen above the water. Nearly all of the ice is under the water.

sea level

**Land and sea**
At the North Pole there is no land. The Pole lies near the middle of the Arctic Ocean. The top layer of the ocean is frozen into ice and snow, which floats on water underneath. The South Pole, or Antarctic, is land, covered by an extremely thick layer of ice.

▶ Icebergs are shaped by the wind and waves.

## Arctic seasons

In the Arctic, it is daylight for most of the summer because the Sun does not set. In winter, it is nearly always dark because the Sun does not rise.

▼ An icebreaker is a ship which cuts a path through ice so that other ships can follow.

**CHATTERBOX**

The bodies of some animals, such as hairy mammoths, which lived thousands of years ago, have been found in the polar ice. Just as a freezer keeps food fresh, ice has stopped these animals from rotting away.

▶ The Poles are home to different kinds of animals. Seals and polar bears live at the North Pole, while many kinds of penguins live at the South Pole.

## Quiz Corner

- Is most of an iceberg above or below sea level?
- What is the area of land at the South Pole called?
- Do polar bears live at the South Pole?
- Is there land at the North Pole?

look at: Land shapes, page 12

# Deserts

Deserts are places where hardly any rain falls and there is almost no water. Living things cannot survive without water, so desert peoples, animals and plants have to make good use of the little water they can find. Often, deserts are hot, dry places, but they can be cold and dry too.

**On the edge of the desert**
Some dry areas have enough rain to grow crops. People and animals can live in these dry places only if it rains every year. Without rain, the land quickly becomes desert. Sometimes, special pipes are laid to bring in water from somewhere else.

**CHATTERBOX**

Desert plants have to work hard to survive! They often store water in their leaves and stems, but they still can't burst into flower until rain eventually falls. Some desert plants also have prickly thorns to stop animals eating them.

▼ Dunes are hills of sand that have been shaped by the wind. These crescent-shaped dunes with long tails are called barchans.

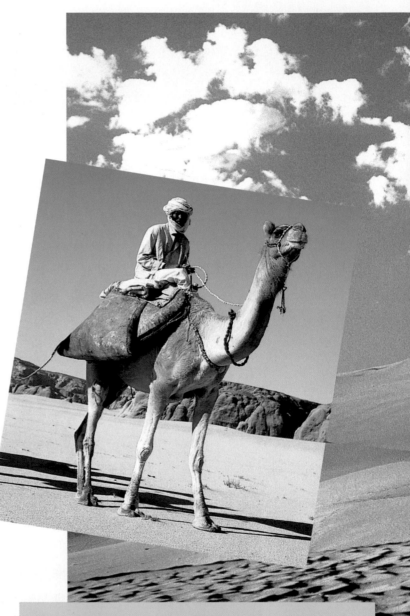

▲ Camels carry people and their loads across the desert. A camel can travel a long way without eating and drinking because it stores food and water in its hump.

**Cold deserts**
The deserts of central Asia are often freezing, especially in winter. Travelling peoples who live in these deserts sleep in tents called yurts.

▼ Yurts are made of tough animal skins and help to keep travelling peoples warm and safe at night.

## Quiz Corner

● Are all deserts hot?

● How do travellers in central Asian deserts keep warm at night?

● How do desert plants and animals survive?

● What is a crescent-shaped dune with a long tail called?

look at: Deserts, page 22

# Grasslands and wetlands

Grasslands are places where there is enough rain for grass to grow, but not enough for many trees to grow. Near the **equator**, grasslands are called savanna. In other cooler places around the world, they have different names, such as prairies, pampas or steppes.

### Grazing the grasslands

Animals that live on grasslands are always on the move, looking for fresh grass to eat. Many large animals live on the grasslands. In Africa, there are wildebeest and antelope, and in South America there are bison. Smaller animals also live on grasslands, gnawing at the roots of the grass and burrowing underground.

◀ Some grasslands in South America are called the pampas. Here farmers graze large herds of cattle that are looked after by cowboys, called gauchos.

## Wetlands

The ground in wetlands is usually wet all the time, although it may dry out a little in the summer. There are wetlands in many countries around the world.

▲ Some plants, such as rice, grow best in wetlands. Often, workers gather the rice plants by hand.

▲ Grass grows quickly, especially if it has just rained. In Africa, grazing animals, such as these waterbuck and impala, move slowly over the grasslands, giving the grass time to grow again behind them.

## Quiz Corner

● Does rice grow best in dry or wet ground?

● What are some of the grasslands in South America called?

● Why are there few trees in grassland areas?

● Where do wildebeest live?

look at: Looking after our Earth, page 28

# Rainforests

In warm, wet parts of Africa, South America, Asia and Australia, there are huge rainforests. The rainforest floor and towering treetops offer different kinds of homes, or **habitats**, for millions of living things. The trees also give out a gas called **oxygen**, which all living things need to survive.

### Rainforest leaves
Many rainforest plants have large leaves that collect water. The leaves of this rubber plant are shaped so that rain will drip off them, fall to the ground and be collected by the roots.

### Parts of a rainforest
Thousands of different kinds of plants and animals live in all parts of a rainforest. The bottom part of a rainforest is called the forest floor, while the tree trunks and taller plants in the middle make up the understorey. The tops of the trees are called the canopy.

▲ The taller trees of this rainforest in Borneo, in Asia, reach up into the sunlight. Other plants and animals live on the warm, dark, forest floor.

Some of the world's biggest poisonous spiders, called tarantulas, live in the South American rainforests. But really their bite is less poisonous than that of many smaller spiders!

## Animal life

Many different animals live in the rainforests of the world, including tigers, porcupines, monkeys, frogs and all different kinds of birds.

## Quiz Corner

- Where do tarantulas live?
- Are there any rainforests in Africa?
- Why do many rainforest plants have large leaves?
- Which gas is made by trees and is also in the air we breathe?

▲ In the rainforests of South America, colourful birds fly among the highest branches. A toucan uses its huge beak to pick berries and nuts from the trees.

27

look at: Deserts, page 22, Grasslands and wetlands, page 24, Rainforests, page 26

# Looking after our Earth

Millions of animals and plants have their homes on Earth. Living things, including people, cannot survive by themselves. We all depend on each other. It is up to us to make sure that the way we live does not harm our **planet**. We can do this by saving the Earth's **resources**, or useful things, and being careful to use only what we need.

### Recycling

We need the Earth's resources to make most of the things we use every day, such as paper, which comes from trees. Instead of throwing things away, we can recycle them, or use them again. This means the Earth's resources will not be used so quickly.

▲ Looking after the Earth is something that we can all do. Bottles, cans and paper can be sorted, ready for recycling.

▲ The Earth is a beautiful place for us to enjoy. Find out more about the area where you live and what people are doing to look after it.

## Energy

Coal, oil and gas are **energy** resources which come from the Earth. By using them sensibly now, we can make sure that there will be enough for people in the future.

### SEE FOR YOURSELF

*Help to look after the Earth by recycling. Save your used cans, bottles and paper and find out where you can take them to be recycled. Check to see whether you can buy recycled items when you go shopping.*

### Quiz Corner

- How can you help to save the Earth's resources?
- What is recycling?
- Name three things that can be recycled.
- Where do coal, gas and oil come from?

# Amazing facts

● The Earth is becoming heavier all the time. Its weight increases by about 25 tonnes every day – that's about the same weight as three African elephants! This extra weight is mostly space dust.

☆ *In northern Norway, the Sun shines all day and all night for about three months of the year.*

● The longest river in the world is the River Nile, in Africa. It is about 6,670km long, running from its source in Burundi to the Mediterranean Sea.

☆ *Did you know that even at night we use sunlight? Moonlight is really the Sun's light reflecting off the Moon's surface.*

● At the equator, days and nights last exactly the same length of time. They are each 12 hours long.

☆ *The Amazon rainforest in South America is the largest in the world. It is home to more kinds of animals than anywhere else on Earth, with many more waiting to be discovered.*

● Coal and oil are called fossil fuels, but do you know why? It's because they are made from fossils, which are the remains of plants and animals that died millions of years ago.

☆ *Did you know that the Atlantic Ocean is growing? Every year, it grows wider by about 5cm, which is about as long as your finger.*

● When water freezes and turns into ice, it expands, or becomes bigger. Fill a plastic beaker with water and cover it with a saucer. Place a heavy weight on top of the saucer and put it in the freezer. Leave it there for 24 hours. Can you see how the ice has grown and forced the saucer to rise?

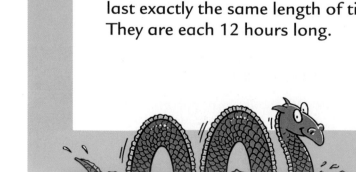

# Glossary

**chemical** A substance that can change things.

**continent** One of the seven large areas of land in the world.

**core** The centre of the Earth.

**crust** The outer layer of the Earth.

**energy** The power to do work.

**equator** An imaginary line round the middle of the Earth.

**erode/erosion** To wear away gradually.

**extinct** No longer alive, or active, anywhere in the world.

**force** The power to make things happen.

**fossil** The remains of an animal or plant turned into stone.

**glacier** A huge, slow-moving river of ice.

**gravity** A **force** that pulls things towards each other.

**habitat** The place where an animal or plant usually lives.

**mantle** The thick layer of **molten** rock below the Earth's **crust**.

**molten** Melted.

**orbit** The path an object takes round a **planet** or star.

**oxygen** One of the gases in air. Animals need oxygen to live.

**planet** A body in space moving round a star.

**pressure** The **force** of one thing pressing against another.

**resource** Something that can be useful.

**temperature** How hot or cold something is.

**tide** The regular rising and falling of the sea.

**trench** A very deep ditch.

**valley** The lower land between hills or mountains.

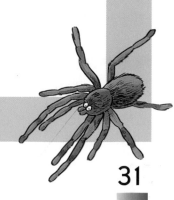

# Index

Published by Two-Can Publishing, 43-45 Dorset Street, London W1U 7NA

© 2001 Two-Can Publishing

For information on Two-Can books and multimedia, call (0)20 7224 2440, fax (0)20 7224 7005, or visit our website at http://www.two-canpublishing.com

Text: Nicola Baxter
Consultant: Keith Lye
Watercolour artwork: Stuart Trotter
Computer artwork: D. Oliver
Commissioned photography: Steve Gorton
Photo research: Dipika Palmer-Jenkins
Editorial Director: Jane Wilsher
Art Director: Carole Orbell
Production Director: Lorraine Estelle
Project Manager: Eljay Yildirim
Editor: Deborah Kespert
Assistant Editors: Julia Hillyard, Claire Yude
Co-edition Editor: Leila Peerun

Hardback ISBN 1-85434-962-7
Paperback ISBN 1-85434-968-6

Dewey Decimal Classification 910

Hardback 2 4 6 8 10 9 7 5 3 1
Paperback 2 4 6 8 10 9 7 5 3 1

A catalogue record for this book is available from the British Library.

Printed in Spain by Graficromo S.A.

Photographic credits: Britstock-IFA (AP Gary Brettnacher) p25tr; Bruce Coleman Ltd (Jens Rydell) p7c, (Steven C Kaufman) p8tr, (Gerald Cubitt) p24-25c; Eye Ubiquitous (Julia Waterlow) p23tr; Steve Gorton p7br, p28; Robert Harding p11r; Hutchison Library (Pern) p24bl; Pictor p13c, p19tr; Planet Earth Pictures p18-19c; Rex Features p10-11c; Tony Stone Images FC, p10b, p15tr, p16b, p17r, p22-23c, p27b, p29tr; Telegraph Colour Library p20-21bc; Zefa p4bl, p9, p12r, p13tl, p14-15c, p17tl, p21tr, p21cr, p22cl, p26-27c.

Title previously published under the Launch Pad Library series